T0210076

THE GUIDE TO INTERNET DEFAMATION AND WEBSITE REMOVAL

PAUL M. STERNBERG
ATTORNEY-AT-LAW
WWW.THEDEFAMATIONATTORNEY.COM

authorHOUSE®

AuthorHouse™
1663 Liberty Drive
Bloomington, IN 47403
www.authorhouse.com
Phone: 1 (800) 839-8640

Published by AuthorHouse 07/26/2019

ISBN: 978-1-7283-1840-0 (sc)
ISBN: 978-1-7283-1839-4 (e)

Library of Congress Control Number: 2019909162

Print information available on the last page.

Paul M. Sternberg, J.D. is in private practice at his own Houston, Texas law firm since 2001. He concentrates his practice in the areas of internet defamation law and business law. Mr. Sternberg is a graduate from the A.B.Freeman School of Business at Tulane University in 1987, and a 1996 graduate from South Texas College of Law in Houston, Texas where he was on the Dean's Honor Roll. Mr. Sternberg, a seasoned entrepreneur, is the author of THE GUIDE TO INTERNET DEFAMATION AND WEBSITE REMOVAL and THE GUIDE TO INVESTING IN COMMERCIAL REAL ESTATE. He has 10 years of experience on representing clients who have been the victims of defamatory cyber-attacks. Mr. Sternberg has developed a reliable blueprint in securing positive solutions in most cases. He has shared his professional knowledge with FOX NEWS and many other media outlets to discuss internet defamation. He is a frequent speaker to attorneys and community groups. He may be reached at www.TheDefamationAttorney.com or his office at 713-789-8120.

CONTENTS

Introduction xv

**Chapter 1: The First Amendment and
Protected Speech in America 1**

Freedom of Speech within the First Amendment vs Freedom of
Expression; the protection the First Amendment offers citizens;
examples of violations of freedom of speech; and interpreting
the amendments for your defamation case.

Chapter 2: What is Defamation? 9

Defamation explained in connection to a violation of free
speech; real-world examples of defamatory statements made
online (social media, chat rooms, group pages, review websites);
introducing fact v. opinions in defamation cases.

Chapter 3: Who is Responsible? 17

Determining the culprit behind a defamatory attack; common
culprits and the motives behind their defamation; identifying
anonymous posters and determining the level of threat; using
cyber investigators to determine the identification of the culprit.

**Chapter 4: Understanding Liability Under the
CDA and the DMCA 25**

Exploring the Communications Decency Act of 1996 and the
Digital Millennium Copyright Act; understanding the liability
of service providers.

Chapter 5: Making the Decision to Sue **34**

Determining whether there's a proper cause for action; anti-SLAPP measures; examples of cases with positive and negative outcomes (notably, the Streisand Effect); cease and desist letters vs filing lawsuits and what you can expect from each.

Chapter 6: Building a Defense **43**

Using truth as the ultimate weapon in your case; statute of limitations (the window of time to respond to defamation); differentiating between public officials and private individuals as it concerns defamation; invited defamation and how it applies to court cases.

Chapter 7: Proof Required for Lawsuit **55**

Proof of malice defined; proof of negligence defined; required evidence and the various forms accepted in court for defamation cases.

Chapter 8: Preparing Your Lawsuit **62**

The process of obtaining a court order explained; solidifying your defense and ensuring minimization of damage from defamation is the priority.

Chapter 9: Removing a Website **68**

What's required to have defamatory comments removed from online; common terms of service violations; real-world examples of terms of service agreements for major publications (including specific defamation violations outlined in agreements).

Conclusion **79**

Briefly covering points made throughout the book and reinforcing proper action required; keys to success during a defamation case; contacting a reputable defamation attorney.

FOREWORD

People and businesses everywhere are under constant threat of online defamation from a range of attackers with unique drives and motives. Victims of defamation have a variety of resources at their disposal to ensure their positive reputation is upheld and the defaming material is removed from its online position (preventing the spread of further damage) ––but without the proper guidance, they may not understand the scope of their situation or the steps required for a positive outcome.

That's where this quick and comprehensive guide will come in handy!

It's easier than ever for perpetrators to commit online defamation using anonymous means or by posting in places that aren't as easy to suppress as forums or websites of the past. Defamation isn't a new threat by any means; however, with the advent of the internet and the increasing importance of online reputations, it's a *growing* threat with mounting repercussions.

Today, people look to a company or organization's online reputation––created by things like customer engagement online, website content, and social media posts––to gain a better understanding of who they are and what they stand for.

Alternatively, people may look to review websites and online reports to determine if they can trust an individual or business to perform at the quality level they claim. While these may not be places that most would think to monitor for defamation attacks, they provide major opportunities for attackers to spread false or defaming messages quickly.

Remaining vigilant against new attacks and responding to defamation quickly are essential in the digital age where getting the word out to an international audience is as easy as pressing 'send.'

Why should I get attorneys involved?

The laws surrounding defamation cases are tricky and are likely to change slightly between each state. For instance, the statute of limitations for defamation usually fall within a 1-2 year time frame. The ability for proper responses and other timely actions must be taken within your Statue of Limitations time frame.

Without the help of attorneys, it's likely that individuals under attack may not develop a thorough case protecting them from future attacks or may fail to meet the criteria required to suppress a defamatory comment online. Defamation lawyers understand the nuances of such a case and can provide real-world insight and share intuitive means of removing attacks and seeking compensation.

Additionally, defamation lawyers are likely to have existing relationships with cyber investigators and other professionals who are needed to eradicate a defamation threat and ensure a client's reputation is upheld against similar attacks in the future.

Why should I look to this book?

In these pages, you'll encounter a thorough examination of defamation attacks, from likely perpetrators and motives to step-by-step instructions on different strategies to resolve them.

This book will help you understand how free speech online applies to individuals in defamation cases and will teach you pitfalls to avoid in your own lawsuit (if that's the route taken). By looking to authentic cases to help illustrate potentially positive or negative results, it instructs readers to make educated decisions in their own cases and equips them with knowledge to protect their reputation online.

When completed, you will have a well-rounded grasp of defamation law as well as a reliable blueprint for removing defamatory content online and restoring (and upholding) your good reputation.

INTRODUCTION

Today, more than 75% of Americans claim to go online every day while over a quarter of citizens report being online "almost constantly." * Some statistics show that half of the entire world-population is connected through social media platforms, discussion forums, online communities, email services or some other form of internet communication.

When we communicate online and share insight into our lives (i.e. through social media posts and blogs), we inevitably develop an *online reputation.*

Sometimes called an e-reputation, the online reputation acts as a first impression to any visitors who encounter websites where companies, products, people, or services hold profiles or post public information (such as Facebook pages, Instagram feeds, Linked In profiles, blogs, Twitter posts, company websites, etc.).

The online reputation encompasses all digital platforms and internet elements that represent an individual or organization online. These elements contribute to how most of the internet views the person or entity—whether that means following posts or avoiding them, trusting a brand or not, purchasing from your company or trying to ward off potential customers, etc.

E-commerce brands, for example, are especially affected by a damaged online reputation since the internet is their source of business. Any loss in reputation will likely cost them credibility, visibility, and certainly sales along the way.

Apart from official branding and content (such as pictures, videos, quotes, social media banners, or ads), an online reputation is often defined by the reactions of web users and visitors.

A poor reputation will likely cost a popular Facebook user many of their friends and likes, damaging personal interactions on a large scale. Businesses with a negative online reputation will lose important customers and money over time. Therefore, even micro acts of defamation can lead to serious repercussions for the person or organization under attack.

As a result, a lot rides on a positive online reputation, and it's wise to keep on top of your digital presence at all times. A single attack against your reputation can turn from a passive comment into a complex problem that cascades down to your audience, customer base, or friend group—ultimately affecting your integrity.

Unfortunately, it's easy to initiate such an online attack today––often even *anonymously*. And once defamatory content is posted and gains traction online, it's hard to contain. The internet is founded on the ability to spread information at a rapid pace, so it's no surprise that businesses and individuals are careful to resolve defamation issues as quickly and thoroughly as possible.

Every attack and the associated level of threat it entails is unique to each defamation case, and not all cases require legal intervention. In fact, certain cases can seemingly backfire or cause unexpected results, such as drawing unnecessary attention to the defamatory comment in question (more on that later in subsequent chapters).

In addition, anyone who is a victim of a defamation attack is subject to an official window of time to formally address their situation before it may no longer stand up in court, and this window differs from state-to-state.

Individuals or organizations under attack should be thorough in their process to identify and rectify any existing defamations, but only after seeking qualified legal help and determining there is probable cause.

In his guide, we'll take readers through a comprehensive approach to identifying the source of defamation, gauging the level of risk, determining who to consult and what actions should be taken to resolve existing issues.

*http://www.pewresearch.org/fact-tank/2018/03/14/about-a-quarter-of-americans-report-going-online-almost-constantly/

CHAPTER 1
THE FIRST AMENDMENT AND PROTECTED SPEECH IN AMERICA

When addressing free speech in America, it's helpful to understand a little about the original laws set into place by our founding fathers and the amendments that make defamation lawsuits possible.

During the late 18th century, American leaders penned an initial draft of a constitution that would govern the people of their newly-declared country. With this liberation from British rule came a new set of standards that were outlined in a document called *The Articles of Confederation and Perpetual Union*.

These initial articles were written at a time when the focus of the country was wartime urgency, and it took a while for people to be comfortable with the idea of a new governing body.

In these articles, the states retained their sovereignty and their independence while Congress took on the roles of treaty-coordinators and commanders of armed forces while also holding the final word on appeal of disputes.

However, these articles were missing a few important components and required restructuring during the Constitutional Convention in 1787 where new federal laws were formed.

The new Constitution would lay down certain basic rights for citizens of the US and help clear up the previous error of appointing states the power to operate like independent countries.

This seemingly weak system was replaced with a stronger form of federal government that consisted of three specific branches: judicial, legislative, and executive. A system of checks and balances were set up through these three new branches that would keep each of the others from gaining too much power.

Shortly after the new Constitution was formed came the first set of amendments that ensured greater freedoms for citizens--the first ten of which are gathered collectively into what we call *The Bill of Rights*. The very first amendment to our nation's Constitution established new rules for citizens, notably free speech and peaceful assembly among other things.

The First Amendment reads:

> "Congress shall make no law respecting an establishment of religion, or prohibiting the free exercise thereof; or abridging the freedom of speech, or of the press; or the right of the

people peaceably to assemble, and to petition
the government for a redress of grievances."

Nestled within that paragraph is the single reference to
"freedom of speech," and, as you can see for yourself, it's
a vague mention without a lot of supporting information
to assist in legal matters.

Many consider free speech a God-given right (or at least
a natural freedom within a progressive society). Free
speech allows citizens to criticize people, places, *their
government* if they choose. The First Amendment protects
people voicing their opinions in face-to-face conversation,
through an email, on a blog, in a text message, or any
other means of communication.

This right ensures that governments cannot censure their
citizens (though this is done frequently in totalitarian
governments), and that citizens can't bring lawsuits
against one another for simply voicing their individual
opinions.

Freedom of speech helps uphold fair trade among
companies and customers, as the latter can openly criticize
businesses who act inappropriately.

Consider a business that makes faulty products or
performs bad services; without the freedom of speech,
their poor quality products will likely reach a multitude
of people before the truth behind their scam is revealed,
costing a lot of unnecessary disappointment and wasted
money. Thanks to free speech, customers can go online and

report when a company sells poor-quality items to warn other potential buyers from making the same mistake.

Free speech also allows citizens to alert other citizens of missteps by any branch of government. Political parties are under constant scrutiny by the public today—and plenty of sources report on political actions in the effort to improve government.

Democracy, literally *a government ruled by the people*, would not get very far without the essential freedom of speech.

It's important to note that the right to speak your mind and voice your opinion without censorship from the US government isn't meant to protect liars and defamers. For example, if Twitter wanted to ban a user who violates the platform's terms of agreement and remove the posts, it's completely in their power to do so.

Making false claims about a company or individual for personal gain, for example, is an offense detailed in many service agreements. False claims can significantly impede companies and businesses, damaging their reputation and the rights of American citizens to engage in a free market along the way.

Defamatory attacks limit the credibility of product and service providers unnecessarily and can filter down negatively to many facets of business.

Free speech is a powerful right that isn't afforded to many people around the world today. It keeps our government in check and ensures the interests and concerns of all citizens can be expressed without fear of punishment. However, the government draws a line when the free speech of one individual negatively affects another individual or business because of a lie.

As we mentioned before, every case of defamation is unique and requires careful inspection to determine if there's proper cause to pursue any legal intervention. Because unearthing an attacker and removing online content can be so complicated, it's likely you'll require the help of cyber investigators and legal professionals (we'll get more into the types of professional help that can discover culprits in subsequent chapters).

Without the help of a qualified legal team, it may be difficult determining the statute of limitations for your case, the specific details of your state's standing on defamation law, the potential for success or failure, and the best plan of action for restoring your reputation.

How does the Freedom of Speech factor into online defamation?

Comments posted online are protected under the same free speech amendment as every other form of communication in America. It is up to the governing bodies of these websites and platforms to define things such as "hate speech" and what may remain on their website.

Free speech laws encourage all citizens to express their explicit opinions and voice concerns to their fellow citizens.

However, defamatory online comments (false, negative statements made over the internet) are unlawful by nature and are subject to persecution in many cases.

In addition, online defamation may be perpetrated under an obscure screenname or else acted out completely anonymously, which may lead the perpetrator to believe they are exempt from punishment.

It's possible that these perpetrators appear on websites and forums leaving comments under an obscure username, use fake or "burner" email addresses to limit how much information is trackable when they sign up, or else employ VPN services to post anonymously from remote locations.

If the attack is proven to be an act of defamation, however, cyber investigators and other legal parties may use lawful tactics to obtain further information to apprehend the perpetrator (such as discovering how long ago they created the associated screenname, where they posted comments geographically, and the unique IP address of their computer).

To track down the attacker, defendants must prove defamation in the online comment in one of two ways: they can prove that the attacker was blatantly negligent about learning the truth behind their own words before posting, or else prove that malice led the attacker to purposefully post false accusations.

Here are a couple of practical examples for further illustration:

If a customer believes a restaurant sells poor-quality pizza that tastes bad, they will likely tell their friends so. They may go onto the restaurant chain's Facebook page and leave a comment explaining just how horrible their pizza is. The customer may leave a Yelp review saying that the place disappointed them, is a waste of money, and that customers should avoid it at all costs.

These comments are protected under the First Amendment as they're expressions of the customer's opinion after purchasing a product (very likely advertised as "the best pizza in town").

On the other hand, if a disgruntled customer leaves comments and reviews stating the managers are embezzling money from the pizza restaurant, and these claims aren't founded in truth, *it's an act of defamation.*

The customer's claim, enacted out of anger and revenge, can cause a lot of damage to the company's reputation. Regardless if the claim of embezzlement is true or not, the restaurant is likely to lose customers and money.

At this point, the pizza restaurant can seek to make up for a blemished reputation and a decrease in sales because the comment was both untruthful and unjust. They would likely assemble a small team of professionals to help prove the defamation, track down the perpetrator, and gauge what legal actions (if any) should be taken for a speedy and painless resolution.

Court cases such as 1919's Supreme Court ruling on *Schenck v. United States* detail how free speech can be abused by the average citizen. Someone who causes panic (and potential danger) by jokingly yelling "fire" in a crowded space isn't protected by the First Amendment. They can be held responsible for any harm created because of their false warning.

There is no constitutional value in false statements, and this is the key to removing any defamatory content from the web and reinstating a positive reputation. False claims or careless errors will not help the advancement of society in the slightest, and there are rules in place to deter this type of attack.

Now that you understand the First Amendment a bit more and how it plays out in an online defamation scenario, we'll go over more explicit examples of defamatory statements in the next chapter.

CHAPTER 2
WHAT IS DEFAMATION?

We talked a little about the differences between opinion and defamation in the last chapter, but this is a broad legal topic that requires more discussion. First, we'll take a closer look at defamation to get a better understanding of how businesses and individuals can come under attack in online scenarios.

LIBEL VS. SLANDER

Dealing with defamation law, it will come in handy to learn a few subject keywords. For instance, you might hear the terms libel and slander used frequently but don't understand the differences between them. Defamation encompasses any statement that has the potential to unjustly damage someone's reputation, and libel and slander are the forms the defamation attacks take.

Defamatory statements made in writing and published where others can see them are considered *libel*. If the defamatory statement is spoken and made public (an argument can be made for YouTube videos) then the statement falls under *slander*. Both forms of defamation are considered a civil wrongdoing, and the person or organization defamed can have online comments removed and, if it's appropriate to the case, may choose to sue for losses under defamation law.

Libel and slander may seem interchangeable when dealing with online defamation, considering people can post anything from pictures and comments to videos and audio tracks. However, it's safe to say most online defamation material is considered libel.

The internet is considered a fixed medium. When something is posted to the internet (no matter if it's a website, a television show, a picture, or a single sentence), it can exist indefinitely.

Let's say that Reddit, the popular news aggregator and discussion website, hosts an online conversation about a particular event that may be useful to future visitors. Top-rated comments (even *defamatory* ones) can be viewed years after they were posted.

Certain sites even keep an online archive of old content, similar to a snapshot of a website's page on any given date and time that can be pulled up again for reference later on down the road.

Unless the defamatory comment is made in a non-capture livestream format then it will likely always go down in the books as libel.

Defamation law is tricky, considering that it deals with both the freedom of speech on one hand and the right to avoid defamation on the other. People should be able to voice their opinions without fear of censorship; also, people shouldn't fear that their hard work, their present success, or reputation will be undermined at the drop of a hat by online defamatory attacks.

Here are a few examples of online defamation to help you better understand:

SOCIAL MEDIA

A while back, a situation arose that concerned Twitter and a case of an individual airing their grievances about a teacher through tweets. In them, the individual (who was upset over their father's replacement by the teacher in question) made comments suggesting that the new teacher was directly responsible for the father's dismissal (which wasn't the case at all).

The comments were seen by many people and the teacher's reputation undoubtedly suffered because of it--though she had done nothing wrong in the first place.

Because there's no evidence to substantiate the claims made on Twitter, and because the false allegations had a negative effect on the teacher in question, the defamer was sued and required to pay a fee of around $100,000.

Whether the individual believed their Twitter comments were true or not hardly mattered. The person they targeted was wrongfully defamed and legally in the right to sue for a damaged reputation.

People use social media to speak their opinions, but they're expected to practice good judgement and avoid letting what they think or believe turn into a wrongful, likely false rant against someone else. Even if the commenter believes what they're saying is a worthy matter of opinion, it can still be tried as a factual statement in court.

This is easier to understand through the above-mentioned example of someone yelling "fire" in a crowded space without proper cause. Imagine a crowded theater on opening night: as a joke, someone in the audience shouts out that the theater is on fire, and all the theatergoers scramble for the nearest exits. More than a few people are hurt in the panic and sent to the hospital.

The person who yelled "fire" may not have meant to cause as much harm as they did, but it doesn't take back the damages some people suffered. Defamation is similar; the culprit behind defamatory statements––who've caused a decline in credibility and reputation of a person or group––will be held responsible for their actions based on the damages accrued by the subject of their attack.

Many social media platforms and websites screen new posts for defamatory or illegal content, but moderators (whether human or AI) don't always pick up on every instance.

Unfortunately, this means defamatory statements are still posted and distributed through feeds on occasion.

CHAT ROOMS

Though chat rooms may not have as many views or receive as much press as social media platforms, they are still major targets for defamation. The traditional "chat room" is an online space where two or more people have chat conversations in real-time. Chat rooms and forums are typical gathering places for genre fans and community questions, but they are susceptible to defamation.

Some of these online forums and chat rooms have moderators who filter what messages can appear on the "wall" or "board" for others to see. However, not all information is filtered and there's plenty of room for someone to enact lasting damage on another's reputation by posting there.

A chat room conversation on local antiques could turn ugly if one of the members calls out Mr. Smith for dealing stolen goods. Perhaps the person posting heard a rumor and decided to use the chat room as the place to call out a colleague's credibility; it's possible they avoid abusing any of the rules set forth by the moderator (or perhaps there is no moderator to immediately intervene), and so the defamatory statements are left available for the world to see.

REVIEW WEBSITES

If you look up online reviews about a restaurant before eating, or if you read product reviews before purchasing an item, you're familiar with the power of the customer's opinion. A handful of poor reviews could significantly cost an establishment or company revenue.

An unhappy customer may decide that calling out the waiter and the kitchen staff for slow service to a manager doesn't cut it. Instead, they decide to write a review that includes false claims of insects found in their food or signs of vermin infestation in the dining room.

Interested diners who look to company reviews will come across such claims and avoid the restaurant at all cost in the future, likely telling friends and acquaintances to avoid it as well.

Such an action can have a snowball effect that can lead from the loss of a few customers to bankruptcy from a lack of sales. A single negative review can influence others to contribute similarly with more bad reviews, leading up to a tremendous setback in customer following, reputation, and finances.

Consumer reports and websites like Yelp are prime targets for such an attack (even though moderators are involved). There are also websites such as Ripoff Report whose purpose is to damage company reputations by hosting negative reviews. Ripoff Report is a privately owned and operated for-profit website that can cause a tremendous harm to a business' reputation and following.

Many of the reviews posted by individuals on websites like Ripoff Report or Consumer Complaints are heated, emotional rants that aim to tear down as much of a company's reputation as they can. Whether founded or unfounded, the poster is usually looking for some kind of relief by posting the report. Though they're a major threat, businesses should know that a lot of the angry rants can be dealt with in an effective manner.

FACT VS OPINION

Just become someone makes an offensive or mean-spirited remark against you online doesn't mean your situation qualifies for legal intervention. Statements that hurt your company or reputation aren't necessarily considered defamation.

However, making false claims against a person or organization and dismissing them as your opinions won't save you in a legal battle, either.

Facts and opinions are often blurred because of language variation and context. The relationship between the two parties involved must be examined to determine if the attack is an actionable offense, among other things.

Although it appears that many defamatory remarks slip through the cracks, it's a good idea to exercise caution when posting online and avoid making vague statements that can be construed as defamation.

In the next chapter, we'll examine the culprits of defamation attacks more closely to help readers identify likely individuals and causes.

CHAPTER 3
WHO IS RESPONSIBLE?

Why would anyone commit defamation in the first place?

There are plenty of reasons that could drive someone to rebel against an individual or company and inflict damage to their reputation. Determining who it was that spread defamation online (sometimes defamers post anonymously) becomes a priority for those looking to sue. A culprit must be discovered for any charges to be filed or any compensation repaid.

In this chapter, we'll explore some of the potential culprits of defamation, how to discover anonymous or difficult-to-track posters, and determining the level of threat to deduce whether any legal action is required.

Determining the Culprit

If you're choosing to sue, then you should understand who it is you're building your case against. Court cases will need to be extremely specific to make any real progress, and a culprit must be identified. A good rule of thumb for online defamation is the "speaker" is always responsible (as opposed to the "publisher" of the website being responsible).

Let's look at the legal case of *Ricci vs. Teamsters Union Local 456 LLC* to paint a clearer picture:

In 2015, a case was filed by Peter Ricci against the Teamsters group of which he was a longtime member. Mr. Ricci reported that he was asked to endorse the union president but declined and was subsequently punished for his choice. For the next decade, Mr. Ricci explains that Teamsters took revenge by frequently firing him from current positions and refusing him new positions he deserved. He claims he was generally disfavored but that the true crime appeared when the Union distributed a newsletter that made defamatory claims against the entire Ricci family––including Mr. Ricci's wife and daughter.

The Union newsletters were also published on a website called theWestChesterNewsletter.com (now defunct) that was hosted on a GoDaddy web server. It was this defamation that came into legal question, but Mr. Ricci did not allege that GoDaddy had any role in creating the defamatory newsletters.

GoDaddy was immune from any potential defamation claims from the Riccis' under a provision of the **Communications Decency Act** of 1996, which states:

> "no provider or user of an interactive computer service shall be treated as the publisher or speaker of any information

provided by another information content
provider." 47 U.S.C. § 230(c)(1)

The Union acted as the speaker in this situation while
GoDaddy was (after a fashion) only a messenger. It's
important to understand the difference between the
Union and GoDaddy as they apply to this situation if you
intend to sue for losses. It will help clarify responsibility
in your own case.

Website owners and authors of defamatory comments
are very rarely the same person, and so you (or hired
professionals) will need to conduct research to uncover
the individual at the source of the attack.

Common Culprits

The attacker in your defamation case is likely to fall under
one of four categories. Knowing these common culprits
may help you identify the originator if it isn't immediately
clear from the defamatory post.

Competitors

It's not uncommon for rival companies (or competitors
of any type) to seek to take down the reputation of their
competitor to boost their own. While they may make
moves to turn away competitors' customers and lower
their business return, any lies they spread that damage
another's reputation is usually liable for legal intervention.
You'll find this type of rivalry and petty attacks more

often in small, local businesses, but it's not impossible for large corporations to act out this way.

Disgruntled Employees

Say an employee has been let go due to situations out of the company's control. They've broken strict rules or gone against their original agreement with the company, and firing is required.

Most make peace with being fired, but there are some who seek revenge. It's possible a recently-fired employee will seek out forums and company group pages to let out steam. It's just as possible that they may spread lies and defamatory statements within these groups to enact their revenge.

Resentful Customers

Imagine that you're selling a cleaning product that claims to remove soap and grime from bathtubs. A customer picks up a bottle of the cleaner and races home to sanitize their bathroom before company comes over.

For some reason, the cleaning product doesn't remove all the grime they expected it to. Already in a frantic mood, now the customer is incited and intends to channel all the rage of their circumstance through an online review. Instead of messaging customer service, they immediately take to review sites or social media to blast the cleaning company. The customer says their products don't work and go as far to claim that it's given them breathing issues and made their animals sick.

It's a highly-undeserved attack (regardless if the product didn't work as effectively as it should) that can cause a lot of potential setbacks.

Extortionists

Extortion is the criminal offense of obtaining money, property, or services from an individual or institution through force or threat. Sometimes a person looking to seek compensation from another person or company will threaten to defame. This reprehensible behavior is more common than you think, and the threat of defaming with untruthful "facts" is illegal whether they even go through with it.

Identifying Anonymous Persons

If you have an idea who's behind defamatory attacks (such as a recently fired employee or a disgruntled customer), it's possible to ask them to sign an affidavit stating they were not involved in the attack.

Guilty parties will likely refuse to sign (since the legal consequences may be severe), which will at least help you determine legitimate grounds to perform a forensic exam of their electronic devices. Uncovering a culprit isn't always as easy as that, though.

Many times, people making defamatory statements will go to great lengths to hide their identity (which makes pinning down a culprit tricky without the help of lawyers and investigators). This will prevent you or your business from obtaining compensation for defamation and may lead to future defamatory attacks.

Cyber attackers may go through VPN (virtual private network) programs, sign up to a forum with fake credentials,

or create burner email addresses and more to ensure anonymity.

Because of constitutional protection of free speech in America, it may seem impossible to discover who the culprit was behind anonymous defamatory attacks. However, if you've come under attack and can't immediately point out a suspect, you can still uncover the culprit with the right professional assistance.

Cyber investigators are one of your most valuable tools for determining the culprit of an online attack. These investigators can obtain the Internet Protocol (IP) addresses of anonymous posters, which is like a computer's unique identification number. From there, they can subpoena internet service providers for subscriber information.

Another way to identify anonymous persons is to subpoena the third-party website hosting the defamatory content. An in-house counsel will then be able to obtain identifying information about the attacker. If the attacker used anonymous or false credentials when signing up (or if none is present) then an IP address will be the most useful information obtained from the third-party website.

At that point, an attorney can discover the internet service provider that was used and find subscriber information for that unique IP address in the time frame of the attack (proving or disproving that the IP address in question was used to make defamatory statements).

Cyber investigators will have to be careful not to overstep their boundaries legally, which is why legal counsel is essential. The limitations of cyber investigators may differ between states, so you'll want to perform research on employable individuals and seek the advice of knowledgeable attorneys.

Blogger Rights

Blogs are popular online platforms for people to express their feelings and for others to comment with their own opinions. We talked a little about fact vs. opinion above, noting that even opinions can qualify as defamatory statements if they make false claims against a person or establishment.

Under defamation law, people who write, publish, or even comment on a blog can face legal difficulties. Many people believe blogging is less reputable than journalism and doesn't adhere to the same laws––but that isn't the case.

The US Supreme Court views the two forms of communication equally, holding the same rights and ability to be sued should defamation arise.

In Chapter 4, we'll discuss the Communications Decency Act and the Digital Millennium Copyright Act more thoroughly and how they help determine responsibility in your case.

CHAPTER 4
UNDERSTANDING LIABILITY UNDER THE CDA AND THE DMCA

We briefly mentioned the Communications Decency Act of 1996 (CDA) in the last chapter and talked a little about how it tends to shift responsibility from websites to the individual poster of comments. It's important to understand the CDA and how it plays out in online defamation scenarios as it will help rule out who is targeted as the culprit in your case.

The CDA was the first major attempt by the United States Congress to regulate pornographic material on the Internet in its earliest days. In the 90s, Congress recognized a need to censure certain information across the new and growing form of communication. They made it a punishable crime to share what was labeled "indecent" material to minors across the internet (up to jail time and hundreds of thousands of dollars in fines).

Congress eventually passed altered versions of the Act, and the final CDA laid a few ground rules for online communication. Besides the attempt to regulate indecent material and obscenity, a section of the Act stated that internet service operators are not to be mistaken for publishers. The "publisher" of online comments is the initial comment poster, and websites are not legally liable for the communications of third parties using their service.

So, if a website owner isn't responsible for defamatory comments posted on their pages or listings, are they ever to blame in a defamation scenario?

This is where a certified legal team with experience in defamation law will step in to help you discover whether a website owner is responsible in your case. However, the rule of thumb is that a website owner isn't responsible for the user-generated material posted to their websites.

The internet is a massive communication network full of posters and commenters, and it's difficult to screen every single statement before it's posted to a website. Most moderators and website owners put standards in place to prevent defamation as best they can (such as thorough terms of service agreements).

The CDA helps protect the value of platforms like Facebook or Twitter and search engines like Google. It discourages blaming the parent site for any statements made by the millions and millions of visiting internet users who are free to speak their minds.

As we'll show you below, overturning the CDA and suing a website for defamatory comments is very difficult to accomplish. It would take new, creative arguments to justify suing a website or website owner since the CDA has been protecting such entities since the dawn of the internet decades ago.

Parker v. Google, Inc

In Parker v. Google, Inc., a case from the early 2000s, a man alleged that the search engine Google archived defamatory content about himself and made that content available via search.

The defamatory messages made about Mr. Parker on a third-party website were displayed by Google as an authorized biography when internet browsers searched his name in the Google query.

According to Mr. Parker's case, he sought to sue Google for multiple violations including defamation, invasion of privacy, racketeering, and negligence among a handful of others. In his lawsuit, Mr. Parker asserted eleven separate claims against Google and some 50,000 "John Doe" defendants who, he asserted, "represent Google's partners through its AdSense and AdWords programs."

The court ruled thus:

> "The mere fact that [the ISP's] system incidentally makes temporary copies of plaintiffs' works does not mean [the ISP] has caused the copying. The court believes that [the ISP's] act of designing or implementing a system that automatically and uniformly

> creates temporary copies of all data sent
> through it is not unlike that of the owner of
> a copying machine who lets the public make
> copies with it... Although copyright is a strict
> liability statute, there should still be some
> element of volition or causation which is
> lacking where a defendant's system is merely
> used to create a copy by a third party."*

Google's system regularly caches or archives information from the web, but doesn't do so in a discriminatory way. Instead, the systems in place capture and store screenshots of what information is already floating around the web.

Google automatically and temporarily stores data––but it does so without human intervention. This means the necessary element of volition is missing from the case.

> "It is clear that [the CDA] § 230 was intended
> to provide immunity for service providers
> like Google on exactly the claims Plaintiff
> raises here."

Nemet Chevrolet, LTD. v. Consumeraffairs.com

Another interesting case that concerns the CDA and online defamation is the case of Nemet Chevrolet, LTD. (the group behind a Virginian dealership) and a review website called ConsumerAffairs.com.

According to Nemet Chevrolet, LTD., the Consumer Affairs review website, which lets new vehicle owners leave comments about their experiences with various dealerships, hosted user complaints about the dealership that violated defamation and other laws.

The people behind Nemet were outraged that internet users posted allegedly false negative reviews of their dealership and the used cars purchased there. They were also upset that the review website had allowed the comments to be published on their website in the first place (stating that they screen posts for defamation before publishing them for others to see).

The representatives of Nemet Chevrolet, LTD. also alleged that the review website had solicited posts from users, organized them in particular categories that would be especially damaging to the dealership, and edited them themselves.

However, the court ruled that the website's behavior wouldn't disqualify them from immunity under the CDA because it did not make them content creators or liable to be sued for the comments.

In addition, the dealership alleged that ConsumerAffairs.com fabricated reviews on their website. Unfortunately, the court found that the allegation was insufficient to move forward, reverting to the original CDA ruling that the responsibility belongs to the initial poster.

The court concluded that the dealership failed to make any perceptible argument on how a website operator "creates" the website content by contacting potential users with questions. In the end, ConsumerAffairs.com was never identified as an information content provider and never tried for defamation.

Hassell v. Bird, and Yelp

The last case we'll look at concerning the Communications Decency Act involves a lawyer suing a former client for poor reviews about his firm left on the famous review website *Yelp*.

The lawyer believed the review on his firm qualified as defamation and requested that Yelp take it down, which a lower court initially ordered the website to do. Yelp was asked to remove the review even though they weren't a party to the lawsuit. The court arrived at this default conclusion because the defendant in the case never appeared in court.

The California Supreme Court sided with Yelp in the end, finding it unlawful to force the company to remove reviews on a legal dispute of which they were not a party. This was the exact purpose of the CDA and its intended protection of companies such as Yelp.

The Digital Millennium Copyright Act (DMCA)

To further help individuals and companies protect against copyright infringement on the internet, the DMCA was penned in 1998 (signed into law by President Bill Clinton) and implements two 1996 treaties of the World Intellectual Property Organization (WIPO).

The purpose of the DMCA was to criminalize the production, use, and dissemination of various technology, devices, or services that are used to circumvent measures controlling access to copyrighted works. In addition, it criminalizes the act of circumventing an access control–– regardless if there is any infringement of copyright associated.

The DMCA amended Title 17 of the United States Code and extended the reach of copyrights while simultaneously limiting the liability of online services providers for copyright infringement by their users.

As we've talked about, responsibility usually passes from a service provider to the individual poster in defamation cases, and the DMCA played a large role in that.

Viacom Inc. v. YouTube, Google Inc.

In a 2007 case, Viacom Inc. filed a lawsuit in the U.S. District Court for the Southern District of New York against YouTube and its corporate parent Google. Viacom claimed copyright infringement and sought more than $1 billion in total damages.

Viacom claimed in their lawsuit that YouTube was engaging in intentional copyright infringement on a massive scale by hosting a contended 160,000 unauthorized clips of Viacom's entertainment programming. To avoid liability, Google relied on the 1998 Digital Millennium Copyright Act's "safe harbor" provision.

In a district ruling, the court acknowledged that YouTube was protected by the DMCA and granted a summary judgement in their favor. Viacom then took their lawsuit to the U.S. Court of Appeals for the Second Circuit.

The federal Second Circuit Court of Appeals vacated the district judge ruling and concluded that Viacom had presented enough evidence against YouTube to warrant a trial. The Court of Appeals determined that the case should not have been thrown out in summary judgment as it had.

However, the court upheld the initial ruling that YouTube was not to be held liable for users who were infringing copyright on their website. The case was eventually sent back to the District Court in New York and the judge issued another order granting summary judgment in favor of YouTube.

Similar to YouTube, the streaming site Veoh established a system where a software processes user-submitted content (without human intervention) and recasts it in a more readily-accessible format for other users to find. Veoh simply selects parameters for their uploading process based on settings from the third-party software.

Because of that, Veoh doesn't actively participate or monitor files that are uploaded by users. The process is automated and is completely at the volition of the website's users.

In the past, music companies have requested for Google to prevent searches and results of copyright-infringing material through takedown notices, but to no avail. Because of the DMCA and the associated loopholes, these websites are protected from copyright takedowns even though some of them are profiting from the violation of copyrights.

As you can see for yourself, challenging websites in lawsuits for hosting defamatory or copyright-infringing content almost never turns out in the plaintiff's favor.

In the next chapter, we'll discuss making the decision to sue as well as potential outcomes and a few factors to consider in your case.

*https://www.courtlistener.com/opinion/2573346/ parker-v-google-inc/

CHAPTER 5
MAKING THE DECISION TO SUE

You have resources at your disposal should you need to sue to make up for any loss in revenue or reputation.

But *should* you sue?

Sometimes, the process of seeking compensation is grueling and may not always end with the resolution people expect it to. The various components in each individual case can vary widely and results may swing in your favor or not. Having an experienced legal team supporting your case in its earliest stages is your best method to ensuring success.

However, if the right steps are taken, and with the help of a qualified professional team, businesses and individuals are able to restore their reputation and make up for monetary losses in court.

The outcome depends on the unique circumstance of the case and the risks involved. Accordingly, you should begin your case with a clear goal and understanding of the potential outcomes.

The Goal

In your case, there must be undisputable proof that defamation has cost you either money or has had a negative impact on your reputation before you seek to sue responsible parties.

If your business has seen steady growth before a defamation attack, but suffered in customer following or sales after an attack, you can usually find numbers to back your right to compensation. A report on earning periods before and after an attack can serve as vital proof in your case.

When gathering proof, you should keep your expectations in mind and determine what your eventual goal is.

Is your mission to have the defamatory comment removed from the internet?

Does the entire forum page contribute to the defamatory claims made against you or your business?

Are you seeking monetary compensation for any losses or damages?

You have to consider your intent before you can determine the scope of your case. Some people may only wish to remove the defamatory contents from a webpage and continue business without any other compensation. Perhaps having the web page or website removed is satisfactory and you have faith enough in your reputation to bounce back from a defamatory attack.

Sometimes an individual or business suffered enough that it becomes difficult for them to envision future success without monetary compensation. In that case, a lawsuit is likely needed.

And at that point, a professional team of attorneys, counsel, and cyber investigators will be your greatest allies, helping you establish a firm case.

Which all leads to the next consideration:

Associated Costs

Those seeking to sue for defamation are wise to weigh out the damages done to their business or reputation and pair it with the potential for further harm in the future. This will make it easier to determine the lengths your team will go to secure a certain amount of compensation.

You'll have to consider the costs of your legal team as well as those people hired on during the investigation to discover the culprit (such as cyber investigators) if one has yet to be identified.

There is also the cost of potential risk should the situation get out of hand (see the Streisand Effect later in this chapter). Legal counsel is essential if you decide to pursue compensation or the removal of defamatory comments from a website as they will help limit risks and mitigate any potentially negative outcomes.

You should ask yourself: *Is the harm done to your reputation equal or greater than the associated costs of pursuing the attacker?*

Some people find a resolution early on by approaching the culprit and attempting to settle the matter over a compromise. Your legal counsel may suggest a cease and desist letter, a useful tactic that may help you avoid an extensive lawsuit.

Cease and Desist Letter

Victims of defamation attacks may be able to take down a negative comment or defamatory statement through a cease and desist letter (which requests that any defamatory comment be removed immediately before legal intervention comes into play).

Many times, the threat of legal action is enough to deter someone from continuing an attack, and it may cause them to remove content without ever having to appear in court. This would save a tremendous amount of time and money for the victim in the end.

Lawsuits such as these involve a lot of paperwork in addition to courtroom appearances and chance of additional negotiations. A successful lawsuit against the defamer will cost them court fees in addition to any amount of compensation asked for.

A court case may defame their own reputation (should that be a concern) and will likely take up much of their time with little-to-no payoff. It will likely make them reconsider their decisions and be more open to the idea of a speedy resolution.

This is the power of the cease and desist letter, which can be an easier alternative to court involvement. It's an opportunity to present the attacker with a chance to avoid a legal fight and to settle the case without hassle.

However, you should understand that once a letter is sent, it's out of your hands and can't be taken back. In some scenarios, the letter may be publicized and potentially draw more attention to the case. The letter or core argument may gain traction out of context, developing its own positive or negative reputation.

A cease and desist letter isn't the solution for every case, but it's an option that anyone facing defamatory attacks should be aware of. The cease and desist letter differs from strategic lawsuits against public participation, which we'll discuss next.

Strategic Lawsuit Against Public Participation (SLAPP)

Employing SLAPPs is something that is illegal in many U.S. jurisdictions on the basis that they prevent freedom of speech. A SLAPP is a tool to silence or harass individuals from criticizing another by making them spend a large sum of money to defend baseless suits. A SLAPP is used to intimidate people by draining their financial resources and rendering them unable to properly speak up and defend their case.

These types of lawsuits require people to pay legal defenses in extensive proceedings until they ultimately abandon their opposition. The defendant is expected to succumb to fear, intimidation, legal expenses, or else become burned out to the point of dropping the case.

SLAPPS may interfere with an organization's ability to operate efficiently (because of excess expenses), causing them a tremendous amount of damage. Repeated litigation against a defendant may cause their costs of liability insurance to increase, further restricting their ability to defend themselves. The goal here is intimidation or else requiring another to spend more money on legal expenses than they can handle (leading to the case being dropped).

Anti-SLAPP laws have been put into place to deter this type of behavior in legal proceedings. These include measures such as penalties for plaintiffs filing lawsuits that are considered frivolous as well as special procedures allowing defendants to request a judge to consider the potential of a SLAPP and possibly dismissing the case as a result.

These laws may come under criticism from those who believe they have been wronged and deserve a barrier-free pursuit of justice. However, anti-SLAPP laws hold up in court today, and many lawyers consistently push for stronger anti-SLAPP laws.

In the Event of a Lawsuit

If you decide to pursue legal intervention, you should understand that keeping a case quiet isn't always easy to pull off. A defamation lawsuit may be a matter of public record, which could allow for additional press coverage on the defamation.

In the lawsuit, the victim of defamation must explicitly state any defamatory comment(s) made against them by the culprit. Pleading the actual statements makes them accessible to the public, and from there open to talk and interpretation.

That may pale in comparison to the damage already made to your reputation, or perhaps there's no worry over a public case as it may actually benefit your position in some way. Still, it is a risk that everyone seeking to open a defamation case should consider.

The Streisand Effect

The "Streisand Effect" is a popular term for a negative outcome for a defamation case, referring specifically to the Barbra Streisand case of the early 2000s. The Hollywood star Barbra Streisand demonstrated how information online can spread quickly in a negative way--even in your attempts to contain.

The singer and actress aimed to suppress sensitive information online and instead broadcasted her case internationally (with serious repercussions). An online archive, called the California Coastal Records Project, photographed the California coastline for its records.

Streisand found the photos and noticed the online collection included shots of her Malibu Mansion for the public to see. She was adamant that these photographs invaded her privacy and should be removed from the online archive. She opened a case to resolve the conflict quickly before word spread further.

This backfired incredibly. Until the lawsuit was filed, her Malibu mansion remained mostly anonymous. Unfortunately for Streisand, the lawsuit brought over a million visitors to the website (as the owner of the archive estimates). In no time at all, her private home's location went from being known by only a handful of people to hundreds of thousands of international visitors to the archive.

Her case was eventually dismissed and worse, the photograph of her mansion was picked up by the widely-distributed Associated Press and printed in news sources around the world, guaranteeing that the location was broadcasted to people around the world.

This is an infamous example of a private case backfiring and gaining more attention from the public, but it's an extreme case.

However, those seeking compensation from a legal case should understand the potential risks involved. It's likely that victims can come to a positive resolution, such as the monetary compensation from the defamed school teacher we talked about earlier.

You should weigh out potential outcomes early on with your legal team and determine the appropriate approach to arrive at a satisfactory resolution.

In Chapter 6, we'll discuss building a case for your lawsuit using truth as an absolute defense to defamation.

CHAPTER 6
BUILDING A DEFENSE

If you're intention is to seek compensation from a defamation attack, you'll need to assemble a qualified professional team and build a bulletproof defense. In a defamation case, your greatest assets are truth and facts, which you can use as spearheads in your case.

Truth is accepted as a complete defense to any defamation claim made against the victim. To win your case, you will have to prove a few things to the court:

- A defamatory comment was made against you or your organization that included false statements

- The statement in question was published or communicated to a third person

- Someone is at fault, and they displayed at least negligence in their mishandling of information

- Yours or your organization's reputation suffered because of the defamatory comment

Truths must be documented and presented alongside defamatory statements in court. Here, you'll counter any false claims called into question during the attack (proving that leaders haven't embezzled money from the company, that the current teacher is not responsible for the dismissal of the old teacher, etc.).

We'll get more into the specific items needed in your defense in the following chapter. For now, let's go over a few critical topics that will come in handy in the event of a defamation attack.

Statute of Limitations

Timing is especially pertinent in a defamation case: lingering on a decision to pursue legal intervention may cost you the available window of time to address the attack.

Deadlines for filing specific types of lawsuits vary between cases and from state-to-state (which is why having a professional legal team to back your case is extremely important to your case's success). These are codified in the statutes of limitations.

The case type doesn't matter: if you miss the statutory deadline set down by your state, the individual you're seeking to sue can request that the court honor the deadline and dismiss your case. It's highly likely that the court will grant the dismissal of the case unless it classifies as a discovery exception (more on that later). Only in rare instances will a court allow for an extension of the filing deadline.

The window of time that victims of an online defamation attack can open a case begins (typically) on the day in which the attacker first posted the defamatory comment(s). You'll have to check with your state (or have your attorney research state deadlines) to determine the specific time window to file civil lawsuits. It's likely your state will have a 1-3-year window to file an official defamation case (see bulleted lists later in this section).

The Single Publication Rule

The "Single Publication Rule" prevents multiple suits from being filed for the same instance of defamation (no matter how many times it gets reprinted). Once a defamatory statement is published, it's original posting date will never reset or change––no matter if the comment appeared in blogs and international news sources after initial publication.

The "Single Publication Rule" implies that the window of time to address grievances from defamation starts the moment a remark is initially made or published online and is subject to limitations set down by each state. If the defamatory statement is later republished, the person under attack doesn't have any legal right to file a new, separate lawsuit.

It's thanks to the rise of mass publication, specifically the internet, that made the "Single Publication Rule" possible. Because so much content is repeated and disseminated to multitudes of people, the rule helps make sure people aren't sued indefinitely for the reappearance of defamatory comments.

Let's consider print publications and how the "Single Publication Rule" is applied: a mass-marketed book will likely take a few days to print, but the first instance of printing starts the clock running. If a defamatory comment is printed in the book somewhere, the very moment the first copy is printed will signal the start of the statute of limitations time frame.

However, if the book was first printed in hardback format but later reprinted in paperback form, the paperback would count as a new publication. Similarly, if the same book were reprinted years later, it would count as a new publication and be subject to a new statute of limitations. The underlying theme here is that each of these new formats or reprintings are intended to reach a new audience.

Internet publications are far different than print publications in terms of how information is distributed and reused. Print publications are considered finite while internet publications are seemingly infinite (because of shifting visibility in search results and quoting/sharing of information).

Additionally, any changes or modifications made to information online will inevitably cause a "republication" that acts as a new publication with a new cause of action (and thus a new statute of limitations).

In the age of the internet, a lot of new questions arise concerning the appearance of online defamation. New websites with better visibility may constitute a new statute of limitations as might the republishing of defamatory articles to new URLs or changing an article title to be more searchable.

In the end, you shouldn't assume that your case is useless if the statute of limitations has passed. It's important to hire legal assistance that can detail your state's exact requirements for a defamation case. Statutes of limitations may even differ between libel and slander cases, but experienced legal counsel will help guide you seamlessly through deadlines.

The "Discovery" Exception

There are a few exceptions to the strict time window surrounding defamation cases, and the most notable is what's called the "discovery" exception or rule. This exception overrules traditional statutes of limitations and deadlines in extremely rare instances.

The "discovery" rule applies to certain situations where the subject of a defamation attack did not come across defamatory statements until a while after they were made (or else too close to the deadline for proper legal action).

While the exception means slightly different things depending on the state, it traditionally stops the statute of limitations from running within its own time frame and instead reverts to a new window that began on the day the plaintiff first came across the defamatory statement.

Potential Extensions for the Statute of Limitations Deadline

If the statute of limitations is preventing you from pursuing your defamation lawsuit, you should consult with your legal team to discover your state's different legislated situations that may increase your window of time. Delaying a statute of limitations' "clock" (as it's called) or else pausing the window of time can help extend the filing deadline.

If someone makes defamatory statements online and damages your reputation but relocates to a different state before any form of a lawsuit can be filed, the rules bend a little bit (considering the defamer has permanently relocated and a new state filing comes into question). Because of this, the time they've been absent from the state isn't likely to be counted toward statutory deadlines. In the defendant's absence (or relocation to another state), the "clock" essentially stops running.

Additionally, if someone's reputation comes under attack while they are still under the age of 18––or else they were legally incapacitated when the statement was made––the "clock" won't begin to run until they reach legal adulthood or declared legally competent and able to defend themselves.

Every state has its own fine print on the statute of limitations, which is why having a team of legal professionals with defamation experience in your state is paramount to success.

Statutes of limitations may prevent you from using the court system, but it may be possible to have defamatory content removed from the internet if you can obtain a written admission from the defamer. Having an attorney or legal team on board in the process will help make your written admission more credible (and increase the likelihood of success outside of the designated window of time to address the problem in court).

While the following limitations are as of March 2016 and subject to change, they serve as general guidelines for determining the statute of limitations in your state:

PAUL M. STERNBERG, ATTORNEY-AT-LAW

One Year Statute of Limitations

- Arizona
- California
- Colorado
- Georgia
- Illinois
- Kansas
- Kentucky
- Louisiana
- Maryland
- Michigan
- Mississippi
- Nebraska
- New Jersey

- New York
- North Carolina
- Ohio
- Oklahoma
- Oregon
- Pennsylvania
- Rhode Island
- Tennessee
- Texas
- Utah
- Virginia
- Washington D.C.

Two Year Statute of Limitations

- Alabama
- Alaska
- Connecticut
- Delaware
- Florida
- Hawaii
- Idaho
- Indiana

- Iowa
- Maine
- Minnesota
- Missouri
- Montana
- Nevada
- North Dakota
- South Carolina

- South Dakota
- West Virginia

Three Year Statute of Limitations

- Arkansas
- Massachusetts
- New Hampshire
- New Mexico
- Vermont
- Washington
- Wisconsin

Public vs Private Cases

In defamation cases, the distinction between a private and a public persona carries a lot of weight. In a defamation claim, public individuals (such as celebrities and political figures) and private individuals (the average citizen) may be required to present differing proof of defamation.

Those individuals who choose to leave private life behind and enter the public arena still retain a few essential privacy rights.

However, certain restrictions are placed on defamation claims involving those who hold a public office or who choose to be in the public eye.

The courts consider public officials to be government employees who appear often under public scrutiny, play a significant role in the government, or those (such as Hollywood celebrities) that live out lives under a spotlight. (look to *Gertz v. Robert Welch, Inc., 418 U.S. 323, 345 (1972)* for more information)

People who are considered public figures are constantly in positions that demand public scrutiny and may have to play out their case a little differently.

For one, public figures are generally considered more capable of defending themselves in court than the average person, and are much better equipped to handle public scrutiny.

Because of this, public figures can't claim defamation unless they prove that defamatory statements are false and that the attacker proved recklessness or disregard for the truth.

The case of *New York Times Co. v. Sullivan* years ago came to a ruling about public officials facing defamation. From this case, the court developed the "malice standard" that's still in effect today.

In this landmark United States Supreme Court case, the court ruled that an act of malice must be proven before reports about public officials are considered defamatory.

New York Times Co v. Sullivan defended free reporting of the civil rights campaign and is one of American history's leading supporting cases for the freedom of the press.

This proof of malice standard asks that all public officials who wish to challenge defamatory remarks made against them prove that the statement in question was false or that the speaker acted in disregard to the truth or any facts in their claim.

Regardless, proof of malice or negligence should be the heart of any argument made against defamatory attacks (we'll touch more on malice and negligence in the following chapter).

Invited Defamation

Something to discuss with your legal counsel before attempting to sue is the topic of "invited defamation" (made famous in cases such as *Johnson v. City of Buckner, 610 S.W.2d 406*). In certain scenarios, these cases can alter the definition of defamation in court and make winning a case tremendously more difficult.

To help illustrate, let's consider that a person is interviewing for a new job––one that will transform their standing in society. They prep appropriately and assemble a list of professional references to present to the hiring manager. Because the applicant has given permission for the prospective employer to contact their references, it's likely that anything references say (good or bad) was done in consent of the applicant.

If the comments made by the reference seem defamatory in nature (perhaps the prospective employer shared details with the applicant), and subsequently cost the applicant the job, they may wish to seek legal intervention in the hopes of eventually attaining the position.

However, most courts won't acknowledge the claim since the applicant consented to the release of the information which cost them their job (past job experience communicated through a reference).

These cases are unique, complicated, and highly-dependent on the present circumstance.

Should you find yourself in a similar situation you should undoubtedly seek the advice of legal counsel (if you haven't already).

Moving on to the next chapter, we'll go over some of the documentation required for defamation cases and explore the integrity of your defense (most notably proof of negligence and proof of malice).

CHAPTER 7
PROOF REQUIRED FOR LAWSUIT

If you make the decision to sue, you must build up a worthy case that doesn't leave any room to question whether your reputation was defamed. As we stated in previous chapters, you will also have to pull together concrete proof that you or your business has suffered monetarily before suing another party for compensation.

As for the proof required against a culprit, you will have to evaluate the situation and learn whether proof of malice or proof of negligence is required.

As you'll see, defamation cases can play out a little differently for public figures than it does for private figures, specifically in terms of the proof required.

Public figures typically must produce proof of malice when presenting a case in court, whereas private individuals can open a lawsuit after only gathering proof of negligence on the culprit's part.

Understanding both will only benefit you as you pursue your own case.

Proof of Malice

We think of "malice" as evil intent, which seems to pair well with defamation attacks. Malice when concerning defamation law actually refers to an attack that was made by someone who knew their statement was false when they wrote it or else acted with reckless disregard for the truth in their statement.

Perhaps a comment was made about you or your organization in reference to a particular event the attacker was a part of. Imagine that a disgruntled employee leaves an online comment that reads something like this:

> "...at last year's holiday party, our boss Mr. Smith announced he would donate half of all charity funds to buy personal computers for top sellers in the company..."

If the employee was present at the party and was told the same announcement as the other attendees—that all the charity funds would be reinvested in the charity—then the other attendees can sign sworn statements testifying the truth.

Maybe the attacker wasn't even present at the gathering but chose to pen their own idea of what the expected announcement would be. The defamatory statement will still cause backlash, even though the poster knew that the statement was a product of their own imagination.

The attacker's state of mind at the time of posting will come into focus in court. The court will more than likely look at the steps the attacker took in posting content (any research, editing, or fact checking in their work) to determine if actual malice was involved.

In a public official's defamation case, they must provide clear and convincing evidence that the attacker in question knew that the information they posted was false or else held serious doubts to the authenticity of the statement.

Unlike the accusation of negligence, malice requires concrete knowledge that the poster knew what they said would be false and damaging (or at least seriously doubted the facts behind their attack).

It isn't enough to prove that the individual who posted defamatory remarks harbored bad feelings for the subject of the post. They must have had distinct knowledge that the comment they made or the material they posted would be both false and damaging.

Additionally, this type of case requires more than proof that the defamer refused to correct the statement after publication or relied on a single biased source when posting; you must produce hard evidence of malice that will uphold in court.

This can be very tricky to pull off (and may be impossible to accomplish thoroughly without a qualified legal team helping). For private individuals, the court only requires proof of negligence as evidence in their defamation case, which, as you'll see below, is a much easier standard to establish than malice.

Proof of Negligence

In a private individual's defamation case, a lawsuit only needs to provide the court proof of negligence on the publisher's (or attacker's) part, which is much easier to accomplish than gathering undisputable proof of malice for the case.

However, certain defamation lawsuits demand a higher standard from private figures––usually if their case is a matter of public concern or importance.

You will have to review your state's specific defamation laws to be certain of your requirements and the documentation that will be needed. This is another reason why having a knowledgeable legal team behind your case will boost your chances of success.

Proof of negligence essentially demands that you prove the poster of defamatory comments failed to use due care to determine the truth of their statement before publishing it online. You must prove to the court that the attacker acted with reckless disregard for the truth of their claim.

You can accomplish this by presenting examples of how the defendant didn't use the appropriate level of care when publishing their statement, essentially recklessly spreading lies about you or your business.

Research will have to prove that the author of defamatory statements did not take every reasonably necessary step to determine their statement was valid. You may have to prove that the steps taken before posting the comment did not include thorough researching, editing, or fact checking.

The defendant would then likely have to produce their own case proving that they *did* conduct an adequate amount of research before publishing the comment, that they had relied on trustworthy sources, that they attempted to verify the truth or fiction behind their belief, and that they followed good journalistic practices.

If the statement made against a private individual is false (and thus defamatory), then it's highly unlikely that they will be able to piece together an adequate defense with these required pieces of evidence.

Let's look back at the example from earlier where an employee posted false information concerning a company announcement. We'll say again that maybe they weren't even in attendance of the holiday party where the information was revealed. Perhaps they only heard another disgruntled employee talk about the announcement and believed a lie about using half of the organization's charity funds for personal computers.

The defamatory statements made against the company will likely cause them a loss in revenue or customer following. Although the poster of these false statements didn't know they were false, they still hurt the company's reputation (and potentially more) simply because they didn't fact-check their statement before posting it.

Proof of Damages and Required Evidence

In addition to the intent behind the post, a defamation case will require proof of damages (or potential for damage) that the defamatory posts incited. This is the key to seeking compensation and it should outline the cost of damages plus the cost required to take the case to court.

As we mentioned before, this can be a statement of quarterly earnings before and after an attack, proving a loss in revenue following defamatory statements. You can tally up how much your company lost in the process and add it to the associated court fees to arrive at a final compensation value.

Gathering evidence may seem like your biggest hurdle yet, but there are many methods of supporting your position if you have the right team backing your case. You can build a case on direct evidence (such as an online "paper" trail or earning reports for the company) or on circumstantial evidence (a series of facts that will indirectly prove another fact, such as testimonies from fellow employees proving that the culprit was aware of the truth before posting comments) or both.

In an online defamation case, it's likely you'll rely on documentary evidence, which is evidence that has been obtained through research and is presented in document form to the court. This can be email threads or print outs of the actual defamatory comment as it appeared online mixed in with personal notes or collected and verified statements from others involved or aware of the situation.

Other forms of evidence may appear in your trial to support your case, namely physical evidence (material objects), demonstrative evidence, or testimonial evidence. Your individual case will determine what evidence is required, however.

Your legal team will likely use a range of methods and processes for obtaining evidence to support your case in court. They may obtain online documents and conduct legal research, consult with other legal experts, and prepare for any potential defenses that may arise to oppose your case.

The importance of a specialized legal team with verified experience in defamation law can't be overstated. They will understand the appropriate processes and will help determine which evidence will uphold in court.

In the next chapter, we'll discuss preparation for your lawsuit and briefly cover a few standard pointers for obtaining a court order and what this means for your defamation case.

CHAPTER 8
PREPARING YOUR LAWSUIT

When preparing your lawsuit, it's easy to get carried away with the details and the potential outcome of the case, or else getting too concerned with revenge instead of a satisfactory resolution.

It's important not to lose focus when setting out to remove defamatory comments made online. Your eventual goal shapes your entire case, from the length of time involved to the type of evidence required from you and your legal team.

Ultimately, your intention in a defamation case should be to minimize the damage done to your reputation and remove any related defamatory statements from the internet. Some victims of an attack may wish to include future costs for repairing their reputation (things like new social media campaigns or blog articles).

A defamation lawsuit isn't a way to secure excessive funds, but instead a way to make up for unjustified defamation to you or your company. It's not uncommon to find people that will treat a civil lawsuit like an eventual payday. This is not the way to view your case, and treating it like a payday has the potential to backfire tremendously.

Taking the steps to repair your reputation shouldn't be driven by revenge or by ambitions to secure large sums of money. You should only seek to repair what has been harmed and as well as prevent the specific event from happening again or costing you in the future.

Drafting a Court Order

If your reputation has been damaged by a defamatory post and you've made the decision to sue to make up for any losses, you'll inevitably need to obtain a court order to enter a trial. However, if you're inexperienced in legal matters (especially defamation law) then obtaining a court order may seem like a massive and confusing undertaking. It's not, and there's plenty of information available on the web or through legal counsel to draft one up correctly.

A court order may be something as simple as marking a date for trial in the appropriate court or as complex as preparing months of past documents and reports into a lengthy statement to bring before a judge. It all depends on your individual case, and a qualified legal team will be able to walk you through the process.

Some cases require more complex court orders or those that act as final or interim orders (temporary orders that specify a limited duration for court to hear out an entire case before coming to a decision). It comes down to your unique circumstance and the scope of your case (say, whether it's made against a single individual in one area or a multi-jurisdictional dispute with multiple people; malice vs. negligence, etc.).

Your legal team will help you determine what elements must be included in your court order, but we'll cover some of the basics later in this section.

At a basic level, the court order will announce exactly who is being brought to trial and for what purposes. You must single out a specific individual for the order to be legitimate (without a culprit, there's not much of a case as there isn't anyone to take responsibility and make up for losses or damages to your reputation).

This means that you must separate the person who posted defamatory comments from the actual website that the defamatory content appeared on (as liability likely passes from the website or website owner to the poster, as made apparent in the Communications Decency Act and various rulings surrounding it).

Remember, the owner of a website doesn't automatically assume responsibility for all content posted on their pages. Certain rules and guidelines are laid out in a terms of service agreement, but not all content will be thoroughly reviewed and filtered, either. Defamatory statements have the potential to slip through the cracks.

In addition, each court order must also explicitly state the defamatory statement that is at the root of the case.

It will likely benefit you to include direct quotes and any website addresses you can find where the defamatory statement appears.

In your attempt to remove comments from a website, it's useful to feature defamatory statements and then explicitly state *how* the statement violated the website's terms. If the court order is made against a poster instead of a website (as is often the case), then this detail will help make it clear to websites when presented with the order why statements must be removed from their pages.

It may also assist you in prompting Google to remove associated false content from its result listings. This means getting rid of any related search results or aggregated content that quotes the defamatory statement and displays it on result listings.

When drafting a court order, you can specify that similar or identical statements found in the future be removed as well. This will assist you take down defamatory statements if they appear in more than one online location or are reprinted.

It's not uncommon for a defamation case to come to a resolution only for the defamed individual or party to discover that the statement has been replicated across other websites and online platforms.

Perhaps someone has had a comment removed from a forum by its moderators for breaking the terms of service agreement. When searching a similar topic months after the case has been settled, you happen to come across another website where the same defamatory information was shared with others.

At that point, if you haven't included a clause that prevents the further dissemination of a similar or identical defamatory statement, then you will have to open a new case to remove future postings (and you'll be at whim to the previously discussed statute of limitations).

To avoid missing deadlines and to thoroughly cover up any associated defamatory comments from your case, legal counsel will help you pen a detailed, comprehensive court order.

Drafting a Court Order

Your attorney or legal team is your strongest asset when drafting up a court order. They will ensure it addresses all the required details of your specific circumstance.

You're free to come up with your own court order, however, it would be tough work to type up a thorough document when you aren't familiar with the specific court your case will appear in and the various laws that surround defamation lawsuits.

In general, the details required in a defamation court order are:

- A clear, explicit representation of the original defamatory statement

- A section which states exactly how the statement violated website terms as well as your proof of negligence or malice

- Proof of a damaged reputation (any hard evidence supporting a drop in customers, following, or revenue because of the defamation)

- Compensation requested as well as a clause for removal of defamation from online sources

- Clause against future "reprinting" of the defamatory statement

If your case requires more details (as proceedings vary depending on each state), your attorney or legal team will assist in drafting up a court order that encompasses the full scope of the resolution.

In the final section, we'll go over common defamation violations laid out in the terms of service agreements for major websites and platforms, as well as discuss online statements that qualify for removal.

CHAPTER 9
REMOVING A WEBSITE

When seeking to correct defamation attacks against you or your company's reputation, it's likely that the resolution will require the removal of defamatory comments from their online positions.

Convincing a website to voluntarily remove any harmful content against your reputation isn't as daunting as it sounds. In fact, most websites have a Terms of Service (ToS) agreement that all posters must sign before leaving any comments, and the ToS will more than likely include a clause that prohibits certain content from being posted on the site.

That doesn't mean that defamatory statements will never appear. Websites may have teams of people (or algorithms and software) that pick through comments and weed out user posts that violate the ToS, but this usually isn't enough to catch all the defamatory cases or other instances of violation that appear. Consider the volume of posts on a platform such as Twitter and the various slang or misspellings defamers may use to post content.

The good news is that court orders can be presented to websites with the intent to remove defamatory comment. The court order should present a clear case with facts of ToS violations against the website in question.

Proving that a commenter posted defamatory statements––in direct opposition to the agreement signed with any given forum or website––is typically the only way to have posted content removed. Otherwise, websites are going against the First Amendment and are likely to cause a world of legal trouble for themselves.

Each website has its own way of dealing with prohibited content, so you and your legal team will have to research into the fine print of the ToS of websites hosting defamatory remarks against you or your company.

Common Terms of Service Violations

Not every terms of service agreement will detail the exact same offenses as other websites, but you can almost guarantee that they will all have a few violations in common. Some of the most standard violations listed in online ToS agreements include:

Illegal activities

For obvious reasons, websites want to shy away from being associated with or allowing the presence of illegal activities to appear on their pages. Most (if not *all*) ToS agreements will mention the dangers of posting illegal content as they would likely face criminal charges themselves for allowing the information to appear.

Malicious/Deceptive Practices

Google's Content Policy outlines a few major malicious or deceptive violations that would qualify for content removal from their listings. They ask that no one transmits viruses, malware, or any other type of malicious code. Google also warns against distributing any content that would cause any damage or interfere with the operation of networks, servers and other Google infrastructures.

Phishing scams and other deceitful practices are explicitly forbidden, and any one of these violations qualifies for content removal.

Hate Speech

While online forums and public spaces leave a lot of room to spread hate or dislike, popular platforms like YouTube clearly state that "hate speech" will not be tolerated. In YouTube's ToS, the moderators state they'll remove any content that promotes violence or hatred against individuals and groups based on characteristics like age, gender, ethnicity, race, religion, disability, nationality, etc.

The terms prohibit any content that encourages violence against individuals based on a lengthy list of attributes appearing within the terms. They don't tolerate any threats at all, and they treat implied calls for violence as real, actionable threats that require removal.

Harassment

Content or behavior that is intended to maliciously harass, threaten, or bully individuals or organizations is not permitted in many ToS. Cyberbullying is a real concern for many forums and websites, and most service agreements not only ban it, but ask users who see content violating this policy to report it immediately so appropriate action can be taken.

Sexually Explicit Material

Many websites ban all explicit material or else require that any material that may be considered explicit is posted with a specific tag. Violating these terms, depending on the content of the post and the common legalities around it, can cause a world of trouble for the poster.

Defamatory Content

Websites don't typically want to get wrapped up in false claims and angry posts or rants about individuals or companies (notable exceptions being websites such as RipOff Report). They seek to uphold the freedom of speech and the right to a clean reputation by only producing honest claims and comments. They will avoid legal trouble by removing defamatory content (once it is presented to them with proof as defamation) and may ban the user from posting again.

Next, we'll look at some specific ToS agreements from popular websites to see verbatim how they address the removal of defamatory content.

Examples of Defamation Violations in Terms of Service Agreements

The following examples offer similar terms of service agreements across differing online mediums: social media platforms, restaurant review sites, and customer feedback forums. Each of these websites or platforms are likely places for online users to post defamatory attacks.

Twitter

In the section "Limitation of Liability," as of February 2019:

> "To the maximum extent permitted by applicable law, the Twitter entities shall not be liable for any indirect, incidental, special consequential or punitive damages, or any loss of profits or revenues, whether incurred directly or indirectly, or any loss of data, use, goodwill, or other intangible losses, resulting from (i) your access to or use of or inability to access or use the services; (ii) any conduct or content of any third party on the services, including without limitation, any defamatory, offensive or illegal conduct of other users or third parties;"

This is the only mention of defamation in the Twitter user agreement. It explicitly states that the platform is not responsible for any defamatory remarks posted. However, they do allow legal requests to remove posts (such as content that allegedly violated laws related to defamation, illegal activities, or national security).

Yelp

The popular review site that connects people to local businesses mentions defamation in their terms of service agreement under "Content, A. Responsibility for Your Content" as of February 2019:

> "You alone are responsible for Your Content, and once published, it cannot always be withdrawn. You assume all risks associated with Your Content, including anyone's reliance on its quality, accuracy, or reliability, or any disclosure by you of information in Your Content that makes you personally identifiable. You represent that you own, or have the necessary permissions to use and authorize the use of Your Content as described herein. You may not imply that Your Content is in any way sponsored or endorsed by Yelp.

> You may expose yourself to liability if, for example, Your Content contains material that is false, intentionally misleading, or defamatory; violates any third-party right, including any copyright, trademark, patent,

> trade secret, moral right, privacy right, right of publicity, or any other intellectual property or proprietary right; contains material that is unlawful, including illegal hate speech or pornography; exploits or otherwise harms minors; or violates or advocates the violation of any law or regulation."

The website again mentions the responsibility of the poster (and the lack of responsibility of the review site) as well as the risk of defamatory statements under their "Restrictions" section:

> "You agree not to, and will not assist, encourage, or enable others to use the Site to: Violate our Content Guidelines, for example, by writing a fake or defamatory review, trading reviews with other businesses, or compensating someone or being compensated to write or remove a review;"

Amazon

Amazon enhances its offerings by allowing customers to review products purchased through a seller on their website. However, this can backfire if a disgruntled customer takes to defamation as revenge for what they deem poor service.

To help minimize the likelihood of defamation on their website, Amazon requires users to sign a user agreement explicitly forbidding it in "Reviews, Comments, Communications, and Other Content."

> "You may post reviews, comments, photos, videos, and other content; send e-cards and other communications; and submit suggestions, ideas, comments, questions, or other information, so long as the content is not illegal, obscene, threatening, defamatory, invasive of privacy, infringing of intellectual property rights (including publicity rights), or otherwise injurious to third parties or objectionable, and does not consist of or contain software viruses, political campaigning, commercial solicitation, chain letters, mass mailings, or any form of "spam" or unsolicited commercial electronic messages."

Removing defamatory content is a lot easier (and typically faster) when the website in question asks users to sign an agreement banning defamation before ever posting. As you'll discover, many websites already have this clause written into their user agreements and need only proof of defamation (apparent in a court order) to consider removing the statements.

Restoring Your Reputation

Once the legal battles are over and you can begin improving on your reputation again, you may ask yourself where to turn to next. What should your next steps be to help put the past behind you and start afresh without criticism or worry over a damaged reputation?

New content and fresh online campaigns will draw more positive attention to you or your company. Any lingering online discussions over the credibility of your reputation will be replaced with new material that highlights positive aspects.

One of the best ways to get the ball rolling on new content is by partnering with a reputation management company. A quality reputation management company will help craft compelling material that can place in top search results and boost credibility to your website or social media page.

Additionally, reputation management companies are well-suited to handle defamation cases as they frequently partner with defamation attorneys and, as a result, have decades of experience in defamation law. Their guidance and know-how will help convert what was once a highly-negative situation into an opportunity to gain back your audience and potentially more followers.

When beginning your case, it might be wise to consult such a company and connect with useful attorneys through referral. In addition to getting an early start to reputation repair, reputation management companies may be able to supply a list of attorneys with proven expertise who are well-suited to your case.

When looking for a credible management company to work with, consider one whose focus is your online reputation.

Some firms and companies offer a mixed bag of resources, which, while seeming like a proactive choice, may impede the progress of repairing your reputation.

These companies will likely divide their time among various outlets to try and boost many areas of your reputation, but the impact on each level will be lower than if the focus were in a single direction. If your online reputation is what's suffering most, then your focus should be on repairing that.

One of the keys to reputation management is staying ahead of the game––that it's easier to contain a negative situation online by addressing problems before they happen. Your reputation company should consistently monitor a variety of channels to ensure they identify and contain any problems before they grow out of control.

Regardless of the company you choose, a reputation management company is a fast track to your renewed reputation and an opportunity to resolve defamation attacks quickly and thoroughly (with the bonus of credible defamation attorney referrals).

* https://digitalexits.
com/3-best-online-reputation-management-companies/

CONCLUSION

There isn't a one-size-fits-all type approach to every defamation case; as we've mentioned, each case is unique and comes with its own specific factors and details that can alter the process.

Your safest bet is to receive help and guidance from qualified legal professionals who have demonstrated a proven track record of success (or at least thorough understanding) of defamation law.

To recap, let's quickly go back over the main points to keep in mind for your case.

The keys to success in a defamation case are:

- Reacting to defamation as quickly as possible to avoid losing the opportunity to counter it (due to a statute of limitations)

- Understanding your case and free speech, and how online defamation is handled in court.

- Hiring an experienced legal team (including cyber investigators and other professional assistance as needed) who are familiar with Defamation Law.

- Determining who is responsible for the defamation attack and whether you should sue the individual for compensation.

- Penning a comprehensive court order that clearly defines elements of your case such as proof of the defamation, proof of its negative effect on your

- reputation, clauses that encompass the full present and future appearance of the defamatory statement.

When attempting to sue or remove online defamation, truth should be the foundation of your case. It's the most powerful opponent to untruthful, defamatory statements in court and should be at the forefront of your court order.

Also, you should aim to minimize the damage done to your reputation and seek only fair compensation for injustice. Remember, you're seeking to restore your reputation to its previous heights and shouldn't just use the opportunity to "boost" your business.

With a legal team at your side, accomplishing this can be easy and painless, and can be done in a timely manner so you can get back on track with peace of mind.

NOTES

NOTES

Printed in the United States
By Bookmasters